Married

&

Loving it

Understanding Keys to Enjoy your Marriage

Brian N Machachc

Contents

ISBN
978-1-77920-788-3
Copyright © 2024 – Brian N Machache

Unless otherwise indicated, all scripture quotations are taken from the Holy Bible, King James Version. Used by permission.

Published by-
Global Word Publishing
569 Mkoba 2, Gweru
Zimbabwe
"Making Maximum. Impact"

Author is contactable on-
Email – brianmachachebooks@gmail.com
Phone - +263775382965

Introduction

The rate of divorce is deeply concerning. Marriage, for many, has become a mere contractual arrangement that can be dissolved at will. This deviates from the intended design of marriage by God. Marriage is a lifelong commitment, where two individuals unite as one. Do not be swayed by external influences. You can cultivate a successful marriage and defy adversity.

All the guidance necessary to nurture a marriage is within the Word of God. This book has been placed in your hands by divine providence to enrich your marital journey. Your union can serve as a beacon of hope for those who doubt the possibility of lifelong commitment.

Your past will never surpass your future. Your marriage will flourish as you deepen your spiritual growth. This book is not a coincidence; delve into each chapter diligently. Meditate on the scriptures provided. The era of enduring marriages is over; it's time to embrace joy. This book offers practical wisdom; ensure you apply all that you learn.

Both you and your partner have roles to fulfill. Together, you will build a family that reflects Christ in a profound manner.

Brian N. Machache

Chapter 1
Enjoying Your
Marriage

I n the special journey of marriage, think of
it as a shared adventure where you and
your partner are not just companions but
storytellers crafting a unique tale. Picture God
as the quiet orchestrator, adding His special
touch to every part of your shared experience.

*"If God isn't part of building your house, you're
working for nothing."* (Psalm 127:1)

Your marriage isn't a chore; it's a canvas
where you paint moments of joy, friendship,
and shared laughter.

In my own marriage journey, I've found
immense happiness. My wife is not a burden
but a wonderful blessing. Our love fills me with
joy. Whenever I feel happy, I remind myself
that God meant marriage to bring joy, not
sadness. Marrying Diana was the best decision
I ever made. I have no regrets; she's my

choice, and I'd choose her again and again. I'm thankful to God for bringing us together. Start each day with joy and end it the same way. Let your kids see your joy and learn from it. Show them how to live joyfully by your example.

"Enjoy life with your wife, all the days of your life." (Ecclesiastes 9:9)

Think of each day as a new page, adding excitement and depth to your story together.

"Be happy with the wife you married when you were young." (Proverbs 5:18)

So, how do you bring brightness to your canvas? Think of small acts of love, like saying kind words or doing thoughtful things.

"Love your wife like you love yourself, and let your wife respect you." (Ephesians 5:33)

A happy heart is key, keeping your relationship strong and lively.

"A cheerful heart is good medicine." (Proverbs 17:22)

Challenges are unexpected turns in your story. Face them together, because what God brings together, no one should tear apart.

"So what God joins together, let no one split apart." (Mark 10:9)

Celebrate successes and share happy moments with each other.

"Celebrate with those who celebrate, and mourn with those who mourn." (Romans 12:15)

When you disagree, be patient and kind. Choose gentle words over harsh ones.

"Speaking gently can calm anger, but harsh words stir it up." (Proverbs 15:1)

Listen carefully before reacting.

"Be quick to listen, slow to speak, and slow to get angry." (James 1:19)

Your joy spreads beyond your relationship, affecting your family and friends.

"Teach your children, and when they're grown, they won't forget." (Proverbs 22:6)

Find joy in simple things together; it strengthens your marriage.

"A cheerful heart makes a cheerful face." (Proverbs 15:13)

Make your home a happy place, using wisdom and understanding as your tools.

"Wisdom builds a house, and understanding makes it secure." (Proverbs 24:3)

Remember, joy is a choice, a result of the Holy Spirit in your lives.

"But the Spirit produces love, joy, peace, patience, kindness, goodness, faithfulness." (Galatians 5:22)

Keep a joyful home. When you believe, God fills your hearts with joy and peace.

"May the God of hope fill you with joy and peace as you trust in him." (Romans 15:13)

May your marriage be a rich source of happiness and love, a beautiful story that unfolds with richness and beauty in each chapter. As you navigate this journey, remember that joy isn't just a fleeting feeling but a conscious choice. It's choosing to find happiness in each other, even in tough times. Cultivate joy in your relationship, letting it enrich your days.

"Always be joyful. Never stop praying. Be thankful in all circumstances, for this is God's will for you who belong to Christ Jesus." (1 Thessalonians 5:16-18)

Let joy be the soundtrack of your journey, heard in shared laughter, warm embraces, and everyday joys. Treasure these moments, as they compose the beautiful melody of your life together.

In marriage, joy is a powerful force, giving strength during tough times. It comes from commitment and love.

"When troubles come your way, consider it an opportunity for great joy. For you know that when your faith is tested, your endurance has a chance to grow." (James 1:2-3)

In your busy life, make room for joyful moments. Dance together, share hobbies - these build a strong marriage.

As you weave joy into your relationship, remember it spreads beyond your home, inspiring others with the power of love. Your joyful marriage is a testament to lasting love in a busy world. May it continue to inspire others.

Chapter 2
Believe In Your Partner

The vital truth to grasp is that God created each of us with purpose and unwavering faith in us. He fashioned us in His image and bestowed upon us His nature.

"And God said, Let us make man in our image, after our likeness: and let them have dominion over the fish of the sea, and over the fowl of the air, and over the cattle, and over all the earth, and over every creeping thing that creepeth upon the earth" (Genesis 1:26 KJV)

If God has faith in you, then there is no reason for you to doubt yourself. Believing in your partner necessitates believing in yourself.

God entrusted Adam with significant responsibilities, illustrating His belief in him. Adam was tasked with naming all creatures, showcasing God's profound trust in humanity. Isn't it remarkable how God believes in His creations?

"And the LORD God formed man of the dust of the ground, and breathed into his nostrils the breath of life; and man became a living soul" (Genesis 2:7 KJV)

"And the LORD God planted a garden eastward in Eden; and there he put the man whom he had formed" (Genesis 2:8 KJV)

If God has such confidence in us, who are we to underestimate those whom He has placed in our lives?

The Book of Genesis shows God's creation of the institution of marriage and His belief in it. God never creates anything in which He lacks faith.

"And the LORD God said, It is not good that the man should be alone; I will make him an help meet for him" (Genesis 2:18 KJV)

God identified the need for companionship and instituted marriage. If marriage was not beneficial, God would not have ordained it.

Many express disbelief in marriage, perhaps due to past failed relationships or abuse. However, one should not let external circumstances shake their faith in what God has ordained and blessed.

One of my daily affirmations is, "I believe in God, I believe in marriage, I believe in the woman that He gave me." When God instituted marriage, it was intended for one man and one woman. God deems one partner sufficient, and we should share that conviction. Polygamy was never God's intention; it arose from humanity's fallen state.

Remember, what you believe ultimately shapes your life. Right beliefs lead to right actions. Choose to align your perspective with God's. It's crucial not to embrace beliefs contrary to God's truth. If God upholds marriage, who are we to doubt it?

Often, Adam's error is highlighted, but we overlook his commendable deeds. Adam's faith in Eve stands out. When he first beheld her, he exclaimed,

"And Adam said, This is now bone of my bones, and flesh of my flesh: she shall be called Woman, because she was taken out of Man" (Genesis 2:23 KJV)

Isn't that powerful? Adam wholeheartedly accepted Eve as his counterpart. Are you still as in love with your partner as Adam was with Eve?

Despite Eve's later transgression, he remained steadfast in his belief in Eve. Throughout his long life, he never took another wife but remained content with Eve, unwavering in his faith in her.

"And all the days that Adam lived were nine hundred and thirty years: and he died" (Genesis 5:5 KJV)

Consider that Adam lived 930 years without seeking another spouse, demonstrating his enduring belief in Eve. It's disheartening that some marriages falter after only a few years due to lack of faith in each other.

Even after Eve's persuasion led to Adam eating the forbidden fruit, he continued to believe in her. While many men might have abandoned their wives for such a transgression, Adam remained steadfast. He lived alongside Eve for many years without encountering marital strife. His unwavering belief in his wife sustained their bond.

Your partner is not flawless, but that should not deter you from believing in them. God placed you in this union for a purpose and offers grace to aid each other's growth.

Remember, affirming what God believes in brings glory to Him. Despite Adam and Eve's fall, God devised a plan for reconciliation, demonstrating His enduring love. John 3:16 exemplifies God's unconditional love and gift of His Son for humanity's redemption.

Just as God loves us unconditionally, love your spouse likewise. Your partner's missteps should not diminish your faith in them.

Believe that your partner is a divine gift, endowed with immense potential. Resist the devil's attempts to undermine your faith in your spouse.

I've learned that everyone possesses the potential for greatness, but negative influences can hinder realization. Your partner harbors great potential; strive to witness their greatness unfold. Refuse to participate in the devil's schemes to destroy your spouse. Despite their mistakes, refrain from condemnation.

The Bible recounts numerous individuals who erred gravely, yet God never wavered in His belief in them. Consider Peter, who denied Jesus thrice but later became a prominent apostle and pillar of the early church.

How you respond to your partner's mistakes shapes their future. Support and belief from those around them enable individuals to rise from their shortcomings.

To believe in your partner, focus not on their weaknesses but on their strengths. Nurture these strengths, and watch what God accomplishes through them.

Understanding God's unconditional love for you and all people enables you to love your spouse similarly. God views all equally; refrain from comparing your spouse unfavorably to others, as God recognizes their inherent value.

The devil often incites comparison, leading some to abandon their partners for perceived greener pastures. However, believe that your partner is complete and possesses all you need in a spouse.

- Believe that your partner satisfies you in every aspect, including intimacy. Reject the devil's lies suggesting others are superior.

- Believe that your partner is attractive and will continue to please you throughout your marriage.
- Believe that your husband is capable of providing for your family's needs.
- Believe that your children are blessings from God.

Chapter 3
Spending Time With Your Partner

The LORD God said, "It isn't good for the man to live alone. I need to make a suitable partner for him." (Genesis 2:18 CEV)

One element often taken from many marriages is the inclination for couples to spend quality time together. Initially, newlyweds aspire to maximize their time together, but this fervor may wane over time if not vigilantly preserved.

The Contemporary English Version of the Bible articulates Genesis 2:18 interestingly, highlighting God's intent for a husband and wife to cohabit and partake in life together.

Spending time together transcends mere physical proximity. It entails a deliberate investment of time and attention in one another.

While physical intimacy is crucial, it should not overshadow other facets of companionship. Marriage encompasses more than physical union.

The significance of having a partner should never be underestimated. Each spouse should endeavor to bring joy to the other daily. Marriage is a personal commitment, not just to family or church, but to each other.

"For this reason, a man will leave his father and mother and be united to his wife, and they will become one flesh." (Genesis 2:24) Reflecting on this underscores the importance of prioritizing time together.

Reflect on who you communicate with most frequently. If it's anyone other than your spouse, it's time for adjustment. Intentionally create time to converse with your partner.

Effective communication is foundational in marriage. Foster the innate desire to converse with your spouse. Share both joys and concerns with each other.

Include your partner in your activities. Whether attending events or watching TV, do it together. Shared experiences enrich marital bonds.

Post-honeymoon outings should continue throughout marriage. Joint activities strengthen the relationship. Money spent together is an investment in marital unity.

Consider the impact of job opportunities on your time together. While financial stability is important, prioritize marital harmony over career advancement.

Economic challenges may necessitate living apart, but strive to reunite. Trust in God's provision for unity, even in foreign lands.

Money is essential, but it should never take precedence over your relationship. Value shared experiences over material wealth.

Balancing work and marriage is feasible. Prioritize quality time with your spouse amid professional obligations.

Even amidst demanding jobs, prioritize bonding with your partner. Simple acts like a bath or massage foster closeness.

Your partner should be your closest confidant. Manage time with other friends to ensure your spouse receives due attention.

Social media can either enhance or harm marital bonds. Transparency in online activity is vital for trust.

Both partners must prioritize spending time together. Create an atmosphere where your partner feels cherished.

How to Create an Environment that Makes Your Partner Want to Be with You Always

1. Let Your Absence Evoke Longing: When you're apart, let your partner feel your absence. Make them miss the warmth of your presence and the joy you bring to their life.

2. Maintain a Cheerful Demeanor: Be the source of positivity in your partner's life. Approach each interaction with a smile and a kind word. Your cheerful disposition will uplift their spirits and make them eager to spend time with you.

3. Avoid Argumentative Topics: Create a safe and harmonious environment by steering clear of contentious subjects. Foster open

communication by discussing matters calmly and respectfully. Encourage healthy dialogue that strengthens your connection rather than driving a wedge between you.

4. Discuss Subjects of Interest to Your Partner: Show genuine interest in your partner's passions and pursuits. Engage in conversations about topics that resonate with them, whether it's their hobbies, career aspirations, or personal goals. By taking an active interest in their world, you demonstrate your love and appreciation for who they are.

5. Listen Attentively: Practice active listening when your partner speaks. Give them your full attention, maintaining eye contact and offering affirming nods to indicate your engagement. Validate their feelings and perspectives, making them feel heard and understood.

6. Physical Closeness Fosters Intimacy: Embrace physical touch as a means of strengthening your emotional connection. Hold hands, cuddle, or engage in gentle caresses that convey love and affection. Physical intimacy creates a deep sense of closeness and reinforces your bond as a couple.

7. Avoid Rushing Intimacy: While physical intimacy is important, prioritize emotional intimacy as well. Take the time to cultivate a strong emotional connection through meaningful conversations and shared experiences. Build anticipation and excitement, savoring the moments leading up to physical intimacy.

8. Express Love Consistently: Shower your partner with love and affection through both words and actions. Express gratitude for their presence in your life and remind them of your unwavering commitment. Small gestures of love, such as heartfelt compliments or surprise tokens of affection, reinforce your bond and make your partner feel cherished.

9. Communicate the Significance of Your Partner's Presence: Let your partner know that their presence enriches your life in countless ways. Express appreciation for the joy, companionship, and support they provide. Affirm their importance in your life, ensuring that they feel valued and cherished at all times.

Why It Is Important to Spend Time Together

1. Mutual prayer and worship deepen spiritual connection.

2. Shared study of the Word enhances spiritual growth.

3. Intimate knowledge of each other strengthens the bond.

4. Joint activities promote unity.

5. Spending time together mitigates temptation.

6. Addressing differences is easier in close proximity.

7. Regular intimacy fosters emotional closeness.

8. Planning together facilitates shared goals.

9. Trust flourishes in the presence of consistent companionship.

Chapter 4
Overcoming Common Marriage Fears

"For God hath not given us the spirit of fear; but of power, and of love, and of a sound mind" (2 Timothy 1:7 KJV)

Fear doesn't originate from God, and He doesn't want it to consume you. God desires your strength and unwavering faith in Him. If you find yourself gripped by fear, remember its source isn't divine, and God doesn't intend it for you.

Fear stands in opposition to faith; it represents belief in the capabilities of the devil. It emerges when one listens to and accepts the enemy's words. Faith, on the other hand, is nurtured through hearing and embracing the Word of God.

"Faith cometh by hearing, and hearing by the word of God" (Romans 10:17 KJV)

Whose voice dominates your marriage? Are you attuned to God's voice or the devil's? Building a successful marriage necessitates faith.

The devil holds no sway over your marriage; you grant him power by succumbing to fear. His initial tactic is to instill fear, gaining control over your marriage if successful.

"Be sober, be vigilant; because your adversary the devil, as a roaring lion, walketh about, seeking whom he may devour" (1 Peter 5:8 KJV)

Though Satan mimics a lion's roar, his aim is to instill fear. Guard against this, as fear isn't aligned with God's will and is detrimental to your marriage. Successful marriages thrive on faith in God, trust in your partner, and belief in oneself.

"For the thing which I greatly feared is come upon me, and that which I was afraid of is come unto me" (Job 3:25 KJV)

You need not live in fear, as what you dread may manifest. Job's fears materialized, but you can dispel such fears in Jesus' name.

"You were in the mind of Jesus when He died; He wants you to have a successful marriage that is full of peace and joy. You are a winning couple, and the devil has no power over your marriage. Stop opening doors for the devil in your marriage by being afraid of him." (Ephesians 4:27)

Your marriage can embody God's intentions. Maintaining faith and trusting God to fulfill His plans for your marriage is paramount. God instituted marriage and remains faithful to ensure its success.

"What are your most common fears in your marriage? It is time you shake those fears off and start believing God."

FEAR OF BEING AFRAID OF YOUR PARTNER

"The fear of man bringeth a snare: but whoso putteth his trust in the LORD shall be safe" (Proverbs 29:25 KJV)

Fear of your spouse contradicts God's desire for you to love each other. Trust that your partner won't harm you. Perceiving your partner as a threat only empowers the devil.

FEAR OF LOSING YOUR PARTNER

"With long life will I satisfy him, and shew him my salvation" (Psalms 91:16 KJV)

Don't fear losing your partner prematurely; God promises longevity. Envision growing old together, cherishing moments with grandchildren.

FEAR OF BARRENNESS

"Thou shalt be blessed above all people: there shall not be male or female barren among you, or among your cattle" (Deuteronomy 7:14 KJV)

Reject fear of infertility; God assures fruitfulness. Remain steadfast in His promises, despite delays in conception.

"I know many people who were very afraid of barrenness to the extent of deciding to have sex before marriage in order to see if there was no bareness. Another couple had to start planning for their wedding soon after the lady conceived. This kind of fear is not good at all. The Lord who promised fruitfulness is faithful."

FEAR OF BEING CHEATED

"Are you afraid of losing your partner to someone else? Some will actually do a lot of funny things in an attempt to try to protect their partners. You don't need to be always checking your partner's phone or asking why your partner was standing with a certain person. You don't even need to have someone watching your partner for you. God is more than enough and more than able to keep your partner for you. You have to surrender your partner to God and leave everything to Him. God is faithful to keep him/her for you."

FEAR OF FAILING TO PLEASE YOUR PARTNER

"I will praise thee; for I am fearfully and wonderfully made: marvellous are thy works; and that my soul knoweth right well" (Psalms 139:14 KJV)

Don't fear inadequacy in pleasing your partner. Recognize your inherent value and trust in God's design. Embrace confidence in your ability to satisfy your partner.

FEAR OF LOSING TASTE FOR YOUR PARTNER

"God was very right when He designed marriage to be for one man and one woman. God made the grace available for the two to please each other even if they live more than hundred years together. The first couple on earth lived several hundred years together and there is no record of them having marriage challenges. You don't have to be afraid, your partner will continue to please you and look more and more attractive to you even after several years together."

FEAR OF FAILING TO RAISE YOUR CHILDREN WELL

"Train up a child in the way he should go: and when he is old, he will not depart from it" (Proverbs 22:6 KJV)

Trust God to provide wisdom for child-rearing. Surrender your children to His care and seek guidance from the Holy Spirit.

FEAR OF STRUGGLING FINANCIALLY

"The silver is mine, and the gold is mine, saith the LORD of hosts" (Haggai 2:8 KJV)

God holds the resources you need. Despite current challenges, believe in improving financial circumstances.

"Your future will be brighter by far than your past" (Job 8:7 CEV)

FEAR OF DIVORCE

"Wherefore they are no more twain, but one flesh. What therefore God hath joined together, let not man put asunder" (Matthew 19:6 KJV)

Reject fear of divorce; trust in God's commitment to your marriage. Face challenges united, growing in love and longevity.

FEAR OF ABUSE

"Are you afraid of losing your freewill in marriage? Are you afraid of being forced to do things that you have never wanted to do? Are you afraid of being controlled? God designed marriage to be run with love. He wants the two people to love each other and to always consider each other. You have to believe that your partner is a selfless person who will not take advantage of you."

FEAR OF LOSING YOUR PASSION FOR GOD

"Are you afraid that your marriage will result in you getting weak in your faith? God designed marriage to be enjoyed with two people who will serve Him together. Your partner is there to help you become all that God has called you for. See yourself growing spiritually in your marriage. Help each other to become more sold out to God. Your faith has to be kept in place. Stay unmoved and unshaken. Keep growing in your faith. Your marriage is the best

Chapter 5
Navigating Misunderstandings In Marriage

The fact that you are a Christian couple doesn't necessarily mean that you will never experience misunderstandings in your marriage. Some arise from differing perspectives, while others stem from the influence of the enemy. Always remember, we have one adversary, and our enemy is the devil. Your spouse is not your foe, and neither is God. God desires the best for your marriage.

The devil despises you, your partner, and your marriage. He opposes everything aligned with God. The good news is that God loves you, your partner, and delights in your marital happiness. That's why it's crucial to pray together as a couple. If your partner isn't saved, trust God for their salvation.

Understanding how to address misunderstandings in marriage is crucial. Opt to handle every situation in alignment with scripture. Remember, neither you nor your partner is perfect. Mistakes will happen, and the devil will attempt to exploit them to undermine your marriage. He thrives when blame is assigned to your partner.

The scripture makes it clear that we should never give the devil a foothold:

"Leave no [such] room or foothold for the devil [give no opportunity to him]" (Ephesians 4:27 AMP)

Always assess whether your actions are resolving the problem or inadvertently inviting the devil in. Never solve one problem by creating another.

Differing viewpoints and occasional offenses are inevitable in marriage. Anger may arise, but exercise caution in managing your emotions.

Remember:

- You and your spouse come from different backgrounds.

- You were raised by different people.

Choose to view marital issues through the lens of understanding. Don't let a single disagreement prompt thoughts of quitting. Dismiss the devil's lies suggesting your marriage is hopeless due to one misunderstanding.

Know when to be silent. Many issues can be resolved simply by remaining quiet. You need not dominate conversations in marriage. When your partner is upset, excessive talking can exacerbate the situation. Stay humble.

"Understand [this], my beloved brethren. Let every man be quick to hear [a ready listener], slow to speak, slow to take offense and to get angry" (James 1:19 AMP)

The Bible advises studying before responding. Allow the Holy Spirit to guide you.

"The mind of the righteous studies how to answer, but the mouth of the wicked pours out evil things" (Proverbs 15:28 AMP)

Know when to broach certain topics. Sensitivity is key. Choose appropriate moments to discuss sensitive matters, avoiding times when your partner is tired or stressed.

Know where to respond. Not every issue warrants a public response. Correcting your partner in public isn't wise. Wait for the right moment, and avoid addressing sensitive matters in the bedroom.

Know when to respond. Respond when you can speak calmly without escalating the situation. Allow your partner to voice their perspective. Avoid hastily expressing your thoughts. Listening attentively can mean a lot.

Know how to respond. Keep your voice calm, and refrain from destructive behavior during misunderstandings. Remember, life goes on after disagreements.

Know who and when to involve others. Some misunderstandings require only the two of you. When external intervention is necessary, choose wisely. Seek guidance from your pastor or a mature believer.

Avoid dwelling on the past. Refrain from resurrecting past grievances during present conflicts. Choose forgiveness and move forward.

Know when to apologize. Apologizing doesn't diminish you. Learn to admit when you're wrong, and sometimes apologize even when you're not.

Be adaptable. Be willing to compromise and consider your partner's perspective.

Exclude children from your misunderstandings. Deal with issues wisely and privately.

Avoid repetition. Address issues once rather than dwelling on them. Your partner is more likely to change when you communicate effectively.

Never grow comfortable with hurting your partner. Seek constructive ways to address issues without causing offense.

Rely on the Holy Spirit for guidance. He is your constant helper.

Here are some negative influences the devil may attempt to exert during misunderstandings:

- Prompting thoughts of self-harm
- Encouraging thoughts of divorce
- Inciting physical confrontation

Choose to love your partner unconditionally. Approach every situation with love, even when correction is necessary.

Chapter 6
Living Out God's Purpose As A Couple

"Two are better off than one, because together they can work more effectively" (Ecclesiastes 4:9 GNB)

Every individual under the sun has a unique assignment from God. Both you and your partner have distinct callings.

Ecclesiastes 4 verse 9 emphasizes the impact couples can have together in serving God. I vividly recall how God used me to reach many people before marriage. While that season was fulfilling, I now witness even greater results in ministry with my supportive spouse by my side.

Consider Joyce Meyer, a renowned figure In Christian ministry. Though her husband remains relatively unseen in public, he played a pivotal role in preparing Joyce for her impactful work. Her television broadcast reaches millions of households daily.

Sometimes, we rush to minister to others while neglecting our primary ministry to our spouses. Your partner's support is crucial for your effectiveness in God's kingdom.

I've yet to encounter a person facing marital challenges who thrives in ministry. The atmosphere at home significantly influences both partners' effectiveness in external endeavors.

I know a gifted evangelist struggling in life and ministry due to lack of spousal support. His wife's unsupportive stance has hindered his progress.

The most perilous adversary isn't distant but resides close to you. Refuse to allow the devil to manipulate you into sabotaging your spouse's unique ministry.

As a teacher of God's Word, I stand as my wife's greatest supporter in her ministry of worship. Likewise, she stands by me as I preach, her silent "amen" amplifying my message.

During the early days of our ministry, exhaustion often overcame me before I preached. Her encouragement fueled my perseverance.

Our mutual support extends beyond vocal affirmation. I facilitate her growth in worship by providing resources and she respects my study time, fostering an environment conducive to spiritual growth.

By exemplifying mutual support in marriage, we can effectively pursue our God-given assignments and foster each other's growth.

Are you aware of your partner's involvement in God's work? You can play a significant role in helping them discover and fulfill their life's purpose.

Sadly, some partners stifle their spouse's talents due to insecurity or fear, hindering their potential.

Many families lack unity in serving the Lord. I've made it my mission to reach out to husbands of non-churchgoing wives, believing in the transformative power of a united household.

Investing in your partner's development is crucial. My wife's academic achievements in ministry do not diminish my role but are cause for celebration.

In marriage, you're not competitors but complements. Create an environment where both flourish and continuously support each other's growth.

Discover each other's strengths and encourage their development. Pray and study the Word together, nurturing spiritual growth.

By supporting each other's God-given assignments, your children will also be inspired to serve God.

Consider the journey of Kenneth and Gloria Copeland, who transformed from unbelievers to powerful preachers, impacting generations.

God can work mightily through united couples. Rise up together and fulfill your divine callings.

In our marriage counseling ministry, my wife's insights have enriched our sessions, making us an unstoppable team.

What are you and your spouse doing together? It's time to unite in serving God.

KEY IMPORTANT TRUTHS

- Collaboration amplifies effectiveness in ministry.
- Support or hindrance depends on spousal involvement.
- Unified effort maximizes impact in God's work.
- Unity in purpose thwarts the devil's schemes.
- Supporting your partner sows seeds for reciprocal support.
- God designed marriage for mutual assistance in fulfilling assignments.
- True marital fulfillment stems from supporting each other's God-given purposes.

Chapter 7
Raising Godly Children In Marriage

"Train up a child in the way he should go: and when he is old, he will not depart from it" (Proverbs 22:6 KJV).

One of the reasons God brings two people together in marriage is for the purpose of raising godly children who resemble Him.

"Didn't the LORD make you one with your wife? In body and spirit, you are his. And what does he want? Godly children from your union. So guard yourself; remain loyal to the wife of your youth" (Malachi 2:15 NLT).

The scripture above has to be the meditation of every couple; God wants you to raise godly children. God never expects you to do something that He has not empowered you for. He expects godly children from you because He has made the grace available for you to achieve that.

THE PERFECT MODEL

Our Heavenly Father is the perfect model of what good parenting is all about. God is our Father, and we are his children. He loves us, his children, with unconditional love, and we have to do the same for our children. We have to love our children.

STAY WITH YOUR CHILDREN

Both parents should stay with their children. You have to raise your children for yourself. No one has the responsibility to raise your children for you. We are living in a world where many children are forced to stay alone after the parents have gone to look for greener pastures. That is not a good thing at all; most children who are raised under such environments become very wild in life. Your children might visit their grandparents, aunties, and uncles during the holidays, but the overall responsibility to raise your children is on you. I personally don't believe in sending my children to a boarding school. In my country, children are at school for 9 months in a year and 3 months holiday. I prefer having more time with my children than the time they have with their teachers. I believe that I am responsible for the parenting of my children and not the teachers.

YOU ALL HAVE A PART TO PLAY

Both the husband and the wife have a part to play in raising godly children. Children have to learn something from their mother and their dad also. In most African homes, the father is very busy to the extent that all child training is left with the mother. That is unhealthy; the input of both is needed.

SPEND TIME WITH YOUR CHILDREN

You can be at home but fail to be with your children. There are so many things that occupy people nowadays like cell phones, television, laptops, etc. You have to create time daily when you drop everything you will be doing and concentrate on your children. Listen to their stories and answer their questions. Have fun with your children.

HAVE CHILDREN THAT YOU CAN MANAGE

Family planning is a good thing. You don't have to keep having children that you cannot take good care of. You have to agree on the number of children to have. Choose the birth control method that is safe for you.

LEAD BY EXAMPLE

In order to raise godly children, parents must model godliness. Children often take on the character of their parents. Parents must be people of character if they are going to raise godly children. Children raised in a loving home by parents with character typically mimic the virtues demonstrated by their parents. In contrast, parents who are not found, who lack self-control in their speech or with their anger, etc., produce the same character in their children. Never tell your children to do anything that you aren't doing yourself.

LIVE THE CHRISTIAN LIFE TOGETHER

Parents have to take the lead in serving God. Pray together – You should have consistent prayer sessions with your children. Teach your children to lead prayer. Study the Word together – After church services, meditate upon the Word of God together as a family. Discuss what you would have learned at church. Read Bible verses together. Go to church together – Never miss church services.

Never stay at home when you should be at church. Consistent church attendance should be your culture. Give together – Teach your children to give. Always give them something to put in the offering basket at church. Let them know the importance of giving to God while they are still young. Win souls together – Winning souls is on the heart of God and it has to be on your heart also as a family. Praise and worship God together – Singing and dancing should not just end at church. You have to do it at home as a family. Remember that as parents, you are the first pastors to your children. Watch Christian content together – Be very selective on what you watch on TV as a family. Worldly music will have a negative impact on your children.

HELP IN IDENTIFYING THEIR GIFTS AND SUPPORT THEM

Your children are not the same. They all have different assignments to accomplish. You have to know your children and support each one of them. Some parents damage their children by trying to train them in a way God didn't wire them. God gave us children who are already uploaded with a unique and specific program like a computer. We can't use software uniquely made for an Apple with a PC. It is the same with children. Some will be wired towards the arts, technology, or serving ministries. It is the job of parents to get to know the way God wired them so they can encourage them in those areas. To know your children, you have to spend more time with them. Stop comparing your children; let them be all that God has designed them to be.

DISCIPLINE YOUR CHILDREN

It is impossible to raise godly children without disciplining them. Since God is the ultimate Father, we must consider how God disciplines us in order to discern how we should discipline our children.

"So don't feel sorry for yourselves. Or have you forgotten how good parents treat children, and that God regards you as his children? My dear child, don't shrug off God's discipline, but don't be crushed by it either. It's the child he loves that he disciplines; the child he embraces, he also corrects. God is educating you; that's why you must never drop out. He's treating you as dear children. This trouble you're in isn't punishment; it's training, the normal

*experience of children. Only irresponsible
parents leave children to fend for themselves.
Would you prefer an irresponsible God? We
respect our own parents for training and not
spoiling us, so why not embrace God's training
so we can truly live? While we were children,
our parents did what seemed best to them. But
God is doing what is best for us, training us to
live God's holy best. At the time, discipline isn't
much fun. It always feels like it's going against
the grain. Later, of course, it pays off
handsomely, for it's the well-trained who find
themselves mature in their relationship with
God"* (Hebrews 12:5-11).

God disciplines us, his children, and every
parent has to do the same. Parents must
initiate various non-punitive disciplines that will
encourage holiness in their children. You have
to instruct, rebuke, and correct your children
out of love. You have to be respected by your
children and not feared. Your children should
know that everything that you do for them is
all for their personal good.

*Withhold not correction from the child: for if
thou beatest him with the rod, he shall not die.
Thou shalt beat him with the rod, and shalt*

deliver his soul from hell. The rod and reproof give wisdom: but a child left to himself bringeth his mother to shame (Proverbs 23:13-15 KJV).

When children are disciplined out of love, they will actually respect you more. The rod will work for a season, and be wise enough to know when the rod is no longer needed.

AVOID PROVOKING YOUR CHILDREN TO ANGER

"Fathers, provoke not your children to anger, lest they be discouraged" (Colossians 3:21 KJV).

It is important for parents not to discipline their children in a way that provokes rebellion. Improper discipline might result in the child rebelling against the parents and against God. Avoid verbally and physically abusing your children. The anger sown is hard to remove and usually the same children who are angered will abuse others.

Never neglect your children, be always there for them. Be their source of encouragement. Stop favoritism, love your children the same. Unwise parenting will breed hatred amongst the children. The children will grow up disliking one another.

Chapter 8
Marriage And Finances

"For ye know the grace of our Lord Jesus Christ, that, though he was rich, yet for your sakes he became poor, that ye through his poverty might be rich" (2 Corinthians 8:9 KJV).

Prosperity is God's will for every couple. We see it right at the beginning, the first couple; Adam and Eve had everything they needed. God made all the provisions available before He created man. Poverty and lack were never on the mind of God; they came as a result of the fall of man. The good news is that Jesus came to deal with the poverty and lack problem. He came to empower us to prosper again. It is important for you to believe God together with your partner for supernatural supplies. God has made everything available for you to prosper.

You have the blessing of God. You are empowered to prosper financially. There is no curse in your blood.

"Blessed be the God and Father of our Lord Jesus Christ, who hath blessed us with all spiritual blessings in heavenly places in Christ" (Ephesians 1:3 KJV).

You have the wisdom of God. The same wisdom that was at work in Jesus is at work in your life. You have the ability to make wise decisions that will bring you profit.

"He has showered his kindness on us, along with all wisdom and understanding" (Ephesians 1:8 NLT).

You have the Spirit of God. He is your ever-present teacher, and He will definitely teach you to prosper.

"But the Comforter, which is the Holy Ghost, whom the Father will send in my name, he shall teach you all things, and bring all things to your remembrance, whatsoever I have said unto you" (John 14:26 KJV).

You have the Word of God that causes you to flourish always.

"But his delight is in the law of the LORD; and in his law doth he meditate day and night. And he shall be like a tree planted by the rivers of water, that bringeth forth his fruit in his season; his leaf also shall not wither; and whatsoever he doeth shall prosper" (Psalm 1:2-3 KJV).

You have the favor of God that causes you to make more than what you worked for.

"It is useless to get up early and stay up late in order to earn a living. God takes care of his own, even while they sleep" (Psalms 127:2 CEV).

You have the right motives that cause God to be more interested in your success.

"[Or] you do ask [God for them] and yet fail to receive, because you ask with wrong purpose and evil, selfish motives. Your intention is [when you get what you desire] to spend it in sensual pleasures" (James 4:3 AMP).

You have the faith of God in you. You can access all the resources that are in God through faith.

"For I say, through the grace given unto me, to every man that is among you, not to think of himself more highly than he ought to think; but to think soberly, according as God hath dealt to every man the measure of faith" (Romans 12:3 KJV).

You have creative ability in your mouth. What you speak is what you get. Living in abundance becomes your life as you speak abundance daily.

"For verily I say unto you, That whosoever shall say unto this mountain, Be thou removed, and be thou cast into the sea; and shall not doubt in his heart, but shall believe that those things which he saith shall come to pass; he shall have whatsoever he saith" (Mark 11:23 KJV).

You have the spirit of excellence that causes everything you touch to look beautiful. Customers will not be able to ignore what you are selling.

You have the character of God in you. You are faithful, reliable, and trustworthy. Your character will attract people to you. Your business will flourish.

The husband as the head of the family has to work hard towards providing for the family. In most cultures, the husband loses respect if he fails to provide for his family.

As a child of God, never allow the worldly cultures to shape your thinking. You can still love and respect your husband even at a time when you are struggling financially. Your support for your husband in difficult times will determine how fast you will come out of that financial crisis.

Nowadays, both the husband and wife can be employed and working together to raise funds for the family. The Bible gives us examples of women who contributed to the incomes of their families: the Proverbs 31 woman (Proverbs 31:10-31) and the Shunammite woman.

"One day Elisha went on to Shunem, where a rich and influential woman lived, who insisted on his eating a meal. Afterward, whenever he passed by, stopped there for a meal. And she said to her husband, "Behold now, I perceive that this is a holy man of God who passes by continually. Let us make a small chamber on the [housetop] and put there for him a bed, a table, a chair, and a lamp. Then whenever he

comes to us, he can go [up the outside stairs and rest] here" (2 Kings 4:8-10 AMP).

There is nothing wrong with both of you doing something to raise income, but it is something that the two of you have to agree on. I recommend that a couple should work towards being self-employed. This will help the couple to spend more time together.

VALUE-BASED BUDGETING

You have to list your priorities in their order as a couple. For example, a couple can have this order of priorities: God, Family, Ministry. Value-based budgeting allows you to align your spending with the things that matter most to you. You take control over where your money is going and choose to spend it on things that align with your faith. It ultimately gives you the opportunity to use your spending as an act of worship towards God.

TAKE CONTROL OF YOUR SPENDING

"And he said to him, Well done, excellent bond servant! Because you have been faithful and trustworthy in a very little [thing], you shall have authority over ten cities" (Luke 19:17 AMP).

When you are faithful with the little, God blesses you with more. God rewards stewardship simply because it honors and pleases him.

- Use money wisely – Invest in properties, houses, and land. Avoid spending too much money on things that depreciate.
- Avoid debt – Never borrow anything that you can live without.
- Have a savings account. Don't use everything that you have.
- Don't forget to support your in-laws.

"If anyone fails to provide for his relatives, and especially for those of his own family, he has disowned the faith [by failing to accompany it with fruits] and is worse than an unbeliever [who performs his obligation in these matters]" (1 Timothy 5:8 AMP).

Always remember that God has made grace available for you to build wealth for the generations to come. Your children can live in abundance because of you.

"Good people will have wealth to leave to their grandchildren, but the wealth of sinners will go to the righteous" (Proverbs 13:22 GNB).

Your finances might not be where you want them today, but never stop believing in a better future that the Lord has for you.

"Your future will be brighter by far than your past" (Job 8:7 CEV).

Chapter 9
Marriage And In-Laws

"Therefore shall a man leave his father and his mother, and shall cleave unto his wife: and they shall be one flesh" (Genesis 2:24 KJV).

Your parents were used by God to bring you on earth; they should never be taken for granted. Your partner's parents are your parents also; they have to be treated in the same way you treat your biological parents. In-laws are a gift from God, and you have to count it as an honor to have them in your life.

WHAT LEAVING YOUR PARENTS AND CLEAVING TO YOUR PARTNER IS ALL ABOUT

Marriage is for adults, people who are mature enough to make key decisions in life. The Bible does not encourage married people to stay with their parents. There is a level of maturity that you will never reach in your married life if you keep staying at the same house with your parents.

You have to be responsible enough to take care of each other without the help of your parents. This does not mean that you no longer have anything to do with your parents. You can stay far from your parents yet remain in constant touch with them. Your parents can be used by God to give you some counsel at certain stages of your marriage, though they shouldn't interfere with the day-to-day running of your marriage. It is not everything about your marriage that your parents should know; that is why staying with your parents is discouraged.

PARENTAL BLESSING

Doing the right things for your parents is needed in life. Parents from both sides have to speak good things about your marriage. You have to avoid doing things that offend your parents. Your in-laws might have their own weaknesses, but you can always find wise ways to relate to them.

- Never raise your voice against your in-laws.
- Never fight with your in-laws.
- Never speak bad things about your in-laws.

- Never curse your in-laws or wish them dead.
- Never abuse your in-laws.
- Never create enmity between your in-laws and your partner.
- Never mock your in-laws.

VISIT YOUR IN-LAWS

Technology has done a wonderful job in making it easy for people to stay in touch, but the impact of phone calls can never be compared with physical visits. You can utilize public holidays to visit them. Your children should also grow up knowing their grandparents.

HONOUR YOUR IN-LAWS

"Honor (esteem and value as precious) your father and your mother-this is the first commandment with a promise" (Ephesians 6:2 AMP).

The Bible does not tell us to honor God-fearing parents only. Your in-laws deserve to be honored even if they don't go to the same church with you. God used them to bring your partner on earth, and that is a great work that they did. Hundreds of children are being aborted in a day, but your in-laws chose to keep your partner alive; they deserve credit for that.

LOVE YOUR IN-LAWS

We are encouraged to love everyone unconditionally. Your in-laws deserve to be loved. Your in-laws are not perfect beings; they might offend you or do some very wicked things in your eyes, but they still need to be loved. You don't change anything by hating your in-laws. The devil celebrates when he sees you doing bad things as a way of revenge towards your in-laws. Your love for your unsaved in-laws can actually lead to their salvation.

PRAY FOR YOUR IN-LAWS

There is a great responsibility upon your life to pray for all people. Your in-laws have to be included in your prayer list. If they are not saved, pray for their salvation and allow God to use you to minister salvation to them.

SUPPORT YOUR IN-LAWS

"If anyone fails to provide for his relatives, and especially for those of his own family, he has

disowned the faith [by failing to accompany it with fruits] and is worse than an unbeliever [who performs his obligation in these matters]" (1 Timothy 5:8 AMP).

Your in-laws need your financial support. Your in-laws might be living in abundance, but what you buy for them will mean something to them. Your in-laws should never starve when you can do something for them.

MAKE THEM FEEL SPECIAL

Celebrate the birthdays of your in-laws and even their marriage anniversaries. Keep sowing the right seeds into the lives of your in-laws. It is wise to celebrate them while they are still alive than when they are gone. It is of no value to bury your in-laws at an expensive cemetery in an expensive casket when you neglected them while they were alive.

UNDERSTANDING DIFFICULT IN-LAWS

I have seen in-laws being used by the devil to destroy marriages. The Word of God makes it clear that the Lord will never allow you to go through what you cannot overcome. The grace of God is available to help you overcome all the attacks that might come from your in-laws.

They might feel that you are not the right person for their child.

They might feel that you are pushing their child away from them.

They might feel that you will stop their child from supporting them financially. They might feel that you are after their child's money.

They might feel that if they make you afraid of them that will be the only way for you to respect them.

You can overcome all this. All you need is to continue doing the right things. You don't lose anything by being good.

Do not let yourself be overcome by evil, but overcome (master) evil with good (Romans 12:21 AMP).

When your in-laws are not saved, they can do anything. Choose to be good to them, your reward is coming. Always discuss with your partner on better ways to relate with your in-laws. You have to be ready to apologize when your in-laws feel that you are wrong.

In some cases, the most important thing is to have your partner's support. You don't have to team up with your parents to destroy your partner. Even when your partner is wrong, find better ways to solve things without involving your parents. Always remember that wisdom is the key to a successful marriage.

Here's the revised text with the simplified words incorporated:

Chapter 10
The Bedroom Side Of Marriage

"Then Adam had intercourse with his wife, and she became pregnant. She bore a son and said, 'By the LORD's help I have gotten a son.' So she named him Cain" (Genesis 4:1 GNB).

The bedroom aspect of marriage is an interesting dimension of marital life. God intended sex to be a source of joy for married couples. Indeed, the first couple created by God engaged in sexual intimacy. Engaging in sexual relations with your spouse is not sinful; it is part of God's design.

Participating in sexual activity within marriage does not diminish your righteousness nor does it render you unacceptable to God. However, it is harmful for a couple to abstain from sexual intimacy and live like siblings.

It's essential to remember that remaining unmarried for life is not inherently sinful. Paul the Apostle remained unmarried until his death, and God accepted him in that state. However, now that you are married, engaging in sexual relations is necessary to pleasing your partner.

"But if you cannot restrain your desires, go ahead and marry---it is better to marry than to burn with passion" (1 Corinthians 7:9 GNB).

God instilled in every individual a desire for sexual intimacy. Having sexual desires is not sinful, but these desires should be fulfilled within the confines of marriage. In marriage, you can enjoy sexual intimacy without compromising your spiritual fulfillment or anointing.

Both spouses have sexual desires, and it's necessary upon both to strive toward satisfying each other in bed. Sexual intimacy should be a selfless endeavor, with each partner working to please the other. This mutual generosity contributes to maximum enjoyment of sex.

Marriage is meant to be savored, not merely endured. Every moment spent in the bedroom should be exciting. Both partners should continuously seek to enhance their sexual relationship, viewing sex as a divine blessing to be relished.

Believe that your spouse possesses everything necessary to please you sexually. Your partner is the best example of beauty/handsomeness, and their body alone should arouse desire in you. Refuse to entertain thoughts that suggest alternatives elsewhere.

Both spouses share responsibility for fostering an environment conducive to pleasurable sex. Avoid statements like, "If you want sex, come and get it." Sexual intimacy is a shared endeavor requiring mutual engagement.

Your mindset influences your physical response. By focusing your thoughts, you can derive enjoyment from every sexual encounter with your partner, even during moments of reduced interest.

Effective communication before, during, and after sex is paramount. Be open about your preferences and receptive to your partner's desires. Willingness to adapt enhances marital harmony and intensifies pleasure.

While sex can occur in various settings, the bedroom is typically the preferred location.

Maintain a clean, well-ventilated bedroom conducive to intimacy. Select lighting that complements both partners' preferences. While nighttime and morning are convenient times for many couples, any time of day is suitable if the atmosphere allows.

Understanding your partner's preferences is crucial for sexual fulfillment. Strive to excite your partner and initiate sex mutually, as this fosters a healthier dynamic. Imbalance in initiation may imply unequal enjoyment.

Sex should never be weaponized in marriage. Avoid using sex as leverage to manipulate your partner or discuss sensitive issues during intimate moments, as it may reduce the mood.

Identify what arouses and what discourages your partner. Continuously engage in activities that please your partner, and never feel ashamed of being vulnerable before them.

Avoid rushing into sex; savor the anticipation. Foreplay can begin outside the bedroom, gradually escalating to intercourse.

"For the wife does not have [exclusive] authority and control over her own body, but the husband [has his rights]; likewise also the

husband does not have [exclusive] authority and control over his body, but the wife [has her rights]" (1 Corinthians 7:4 AMP).

Your body belongs to your partner; enjoy their touch and reciprocate during foreplay. Take time to explore each other's bodies, stimulating sensitive areas and providing verbal encouragement.

Foreplay prepares both partners for intercourse, facilitating natural lubrication. Penetration should be gentle initially, gradually increasing in intensity.

Agree on sexual positions that allow mutual participation, avoiding exerting excessive weight on your partner.

Men often reach orgasm faster than women, necessitating patience and self-control from husbands. Women can experience multiple orgasms, so understanding and attentiveness are crucial.

After intercourse, bathing together can enhance intimacy and hygiene. Maintaining cleanliness and fresh breath contributes to a more enjoyable experience.

"So don't refuse sex to each other, unless you agree not to have sex for a little while, in order to spend time in prayer. Then Satan won't be able to tempt you because of your lack of self-control" (1 Corinthians 7:5 CEV).

Refusing sex to your partner, except for agreed-upon reasons such as health concerns or prayer, is unwise. Be attuned to your partner's needs and communicate openly to maintain a healthy sexual relationship.

Avoid making one-sided decisions regarding sexual frequency; prioritize mutual satisfaction and understanding. Consistently nurturing your partner's sexual fulfillment fosters a fulfilling marital bond.

If your partner is fatigued, demonstrate care and support through acts like bathing together or offering massages. Denying your partner sex after they've fulfilled their responsibilities can be sinful and should be repented of.

Continue sowing seeds of love in your marriage, cultivating intimacy and mutual satisfaction. Reflect on whether your love for each other is growing or waning, and make joint efforts to reignite passion and devotion

Chapter 11
Believing God For The Salvation Of An Unsaved Partner

"If it seems evil to you to serve the LORD, choose for yourselves this day whom you will serve: whether the gods which your fathers served that were on the other side of the flood, or the gods of the Amorites, in whose land you dwell. But as for me and my house, we will serve the LORD." (Joshua 24:15 KJV)

The declaration of Joshua must also be your declaration. You must serve God together with your spouse and children. If one of you is not saved, that is an open door that the devil will always try to capitalize on.

The devil doesn't want to see you happy in marriage. He hates you and wants to see you crying every day. On the other hand, God wants you to enjoy heaven on earth. He wants you to enjoy and not to endure.

"Do not be unequally yoked with unbelievers [do not make mismated alliances with them or come under a different yoke with them, inconsistent with your faith]. For what partnership have right living and right standing with God with iniquity and lawlessness? Or how can light have fellowship with darkness?" (2 Corinthians 6:14 AMP)

Our God was right when He discouraged believers from marrying unbelievers. Many people blame God for their marriage problems, yet they chose their partners themselves. I am not here to condemn anyone who married an unbeliever; I am here to encourage you to believe God for the salvation of your partner.

REASONS WHY MANY END UP IN UNEQUAL YOKES:

- Impatience
- Immaturity
- Carelessness
- Lack of vision
- Carnality
- Bad influences
- Lack of proper teaching

Some consciously married unbelievers, while others married someone who appeared to be a believer but wasn't truly. Remember, people might do anything just to convince someone to marry them.

Another group includes those who were both believers when they got married, only for one to backslide along the way. Some of these individuals become radical sinners despite knowing the truth, choosing to disobey God.

In some cases, both partners were unbelievers when they got married. Kenneth and Gloria Copeland were both sinners when they married. Later, they got saved and became wonderful servants of God, doing amazing work in His kingdom.

There is no situation that is hopeless before the Lord. Even the worst sinners can still come to the Lord. Having been involved in practical ministry for the past 15 years, I have seen radical sinners coming to the Lord. Never stop believing that your spouse will come to the Lord.

It was disturbing to hear two Christian women say they enjoy having unsaved husbands because they wanted their freedom to socialize. They claimed that a Christian husband is always at home, leading to more conflicts. It's essential to desire to see your partner serving God. It is a great blessing when you both worship God together.

I led another man to Christ a few years ago. His wife was already saved and attending another church, but he chose to join ours due to differences in worship styles. I was comfortable with him attending his wife's church, but he insisted on ours. Unfortunately, his wife resisted, leading to his backsliding into alcoholism and smoking.

I am still believing God to restore this man, though it will not be easy. This situation serves as a reminder never to take for granted the opportunity to have your partner serving God with you. I also blame the pastor of this lady for not making efforts to encourage her to join her husband's church, despite understanding the situation.

Refuse to be the one hindering your partner from coming to the Lord. The way you conduct yourself at home can either have a positive or negative impact on your partner's salvation.

When I see a spouse attending church alone, I always make an effort to reach out to the other partner. It saddens me that most believing spouses are doing nothing to get their partner saved. All they say is, "My husband/wife is difficult and will never change." Words are powerful; speak the right words over your marriage and partner.

IN LIKE MANNER, you married women, be submissive to your own husbands [subordinate yourselves as secondary and dependent on them, and adapt to them], so that even if any do not obey the Word [of God], they may be won over not by discussion but by the godly lives of their wives. (1 Peter 3:1 AMP)

The conduct of the saved spouse can either convince the other to come to the Lord or push them further away. If you are saved, remember that you represent Christ in your marriage. Are you representing Him well?

There are many reasons why it is crucial to believe God for the salvation of your spouse:

- The unbelieving spouse might divert your attention from God.

- The unbelieving spouse might hinder you from accomplishing your God-given assignment.
- The unbelieving spouse might cheat and introduce STIs into the home.
- There are high chances of divorce.
- Children might be exposed to an unhealthy environment.

Here are some ways to help your partner come to the Lord. The Holy Spirit will guide you on what will work best in your situation:

- Pray for your partner—bind every spirit hindering their salvation.
- Share Christ with them.
- Live an exemplary life—preach Christ through your actions.
- Love/honor your partner unconditionally.
- Invite your partner to church.
- Involve your partner in your home prayer times.
- Introduce your partner to your pastors.

"And when he had found him, he brought him to Antioch. So it was that for a whole year they assembled with the church and taught a great many people. And the disciples were first called Christians in Antioch." (Acts 11:26 KJV)

The believers were first called Christians at Antioch because they spoke, acted, and lived like Christ. Live like Jesus at home, and you will convince your partner to serve God with you.

Never condemn or judge your partner. Let them know that they are loved by God. Stop telling your husband/wife that they are going to hell.

You need to know how to lead someone to Christ because you might be the one to lead your partner. Here are simple steps to lead someone into the prayer of salvation:

Romans 10:9-10, John 1:12

- Acknowledge sin and inability to save oneself.
- Believe in Jesus and the finished work of the cross.
- Confess the Lordship of Jesus.

The Prayer:

"Lord Jesus, I come to You today. I acknowledge that I am a sinner and cannot save myself. I believe in Jesus and the finished work of the cross. I confess that Jesus is Lord,

and I accept Him into my heart. Thank You,
Father, for saving me, in Jesus' name. Amen. "

If your partner makes this prayer, they are
saved. You can then help them grow in the
Lord. Read the Bible together, pray together,
and attend church together. Don't expect
immediate change in every area; some
changes will come instantly, while others will
be gradual.

One of the leading American pastors, Jerry
Savelle, was influenced by his wife to join
church. He later got saved and became a
wonderful teacher of the Word of God. See
your partner becoming great in the Lord.

You are an anointed person. Believe that every
spirit causing your partner to deny Christ will
bow in Jesus' name. The Holy Spirit is at work.
As you share the same bed with your spouse,
believe that the Lord is touching their heart.

You must be fully convinced that your presence
in your partner's life means something great to
them. Visualize yourself sitting together with
your partner in church. How you conduct
yourself in the presence of your in-laws and

family will also help convince your partner that you are sent from the Lord.

www.ingramcontent.com/pod-product-compliance
Lightning Source LLC
Chambersburg PA
CBHW072046040426
42447CB00012BB/3043